Edible Wild Plants

Todd Telander

FALCONGUIDES

GUILFORD, CONNECTICUT
HELENA, MONTANA
AN IMPRINT OF GLOBE PEQUOT PRESS

To my wife, Kirsten, my children, Miles and Oliver, and my parents, all of whom have supported and encouraged me through the years.

Special thanks to Gary Lenz for sharing his knowledge of plants.

To buy books in quantity for corporate use or incentives, call **(800) 962-0973** or e-mail **premiums@GlobePequot.com.**

FSC
www.fsc.org
MIX
Paper from
responsible sources
FSC® C005010

FALCONGUIDES®

Text design: Sheryl P. Kober
Layout: Sue Murray
Project editor: David Legere

Library of Congress Cataloging-in-Publication Data is available on file.

ISBN 978-0-7627-7421-0

Printed in the United States of America
10 9 8 7 6 5 4 3 2

Contents

Introduction

Learning about edible wild plants not only will provide you with some extra food but also will inevitably lead you on a path of discovery about the natural world and our connection to it. Many of the plants we walk past every day, see as ornamentals, or destroy as weeds are indeed edible, delicious, and filled with nutrients. It takes only a few moments and some thoughtful observation to learn enough about a plant to know its value as an edible, but you can spend years delving deeper into its life cycle, place in the ecosystem, and history of use by native peoples. So, the next time you pull a "weed" from your garden, chances are you could be eating it for lunch.

This guide covers ninety of some of the more common edible wild plants in the United States. Of course, you can learn about many more by reading comprehensive field guides, taking courses taught by experts in the field, or studying native cultures. Plants included in this guide represent a diversity of families, environments, and regions. From algae to flowering plants, deserts to the sea, an outdoor buffet awaits!

Note: Collectors should inquire regarding local regulations on public lands prior to collecting wild plants, especially in national parks, where such actions are generally prohibited or limited by type and quantity.

Notes about the Entries

Order

The order of plants listed in this guide is based loosely on phylogenetic relationships, from the simpler, early plants to more complex, later plants. The algae are unicellular plants that grow only in water because they lack supportive stems and a vascular system. The ferns and horsetails are early land plants that lack seeds and reproduce instead by spores. Gymnosperms, such as the pines, lack flowers and have seeds that are borne in cones. The angiosperms are the largest, most familiar group, with flowers and seeds borne in some kind of fruit.

Names

The common name(s) as well as the scientific name are included for each entry. Because common names tend to vary regionally, or there may be more than one common name for each species (some plants have over a dozen common names), the universally accepted scientific name of genus and species (such as *Rumex crispus* for curly dock) is a more reliable identifier. Also, one can often learn interesting facts about a plant from the English translation of its Latin name. For instance, the generic name *Rumex* is Latin for a kind of sorrel, and *crispus* means "wavy" or "curly," describing the curled leaf margins of the curly dock.

Families

Plants are grouped into families based on similar structures, growth habits, and common ancestry. After you are familiar with some of the more common plant families and their shared characteristics, you can often place an unfamiliar plant into a family, which will reduce your search to a smaller group. For example, if you find an herbaceous plant with a five-petaled flower; alternate, serrate leaves; and a prickled stem, you might first look in the family Rosaceae (which includes wild roses, blackberries, and cherries) and narrow your search from there. You may find a diagram for leaf shapes, margins, and terms on page 1.

Size

The size given for each plant is the maximum size you are likely to find and occurs when environmental conditions are ideal and you are looking at a fully mature specimen. If conditions are less favorable, or if you find a specimen early in its growth cycle, the plant may be much smaller.

Range

The range of each species can be very wide, such as across the entire United States, or limited to a certain region, such as the Southwest or Northeast. Within a plant's range, it is important to note the specific habitat where it occurs.

Season

The season listed is when the plant is actively growing. If there are specific times when an important plant part, such as flowers or fruit, is available, those times are also indicated.

Habitat

A plant's habitat is an excellent key to identification. Although some nonnative, invasive plants grow almost anywhere, most have fairly specific environments where they prosper. Factors such as soil conditions, temperature, water availability, elevation, and surrounding vegetation all play an important role in a plant's ability to survive. You won't find wild rice growing in the desert or catclaw growing in swamps. One exception is plants that are used as ornamentals, which may be found far from their natural habitat.

Descriptions

The descriptions give the basic structure and growth habit of each plant, including its life cycle, stem shape, leaf shape and arrangement, flower details, kinds of seed or fruit, and root form. They are not comprehensive descriptions but are designed to include essential information to help in your identification process. Other clues may include hairiness (or lack or hairs), spines, textures, and odors. Some plants may be obvious and unique, whereas others are so similar that they may require the use of additional references to ensure proper identification.

Uses

This book is designed primarily to address the edibility of wild plants, although in some cases medicinal qualities or structural uses are also noted because they may be of particular interest. Often, the timing of your harvest is crucial to how a plant part will taste, particularly with leaves, which often become quite tough or bitter if picked too late or from an older part of the plant. Unripe fruits are usually unpalatable, and roots and tubers taken during the growth cycle of the above-ground plant will be small and fibrous. Some plants have parts that are delicious eaten raw, whereas others have parts that must be cooked (either to have better flavor and texture or to remove toxins). **Always consult an expert before eating any wild plant because some that look like edibles are highly poisonous.**

Illustrations

The illustrations are designed to show the most important structures to help in identification. Usually these include a section of the stem with leaves, flowers, and fruit and sometimes the roots or tubers. For expediency, sometimes I have shown the plant with flowers and fruit present at the same time, although this may not always occur naturally. Also note that leaf shapes may vary and that those illustrated are only a representative of those mentioned in the text.

Flower Parts

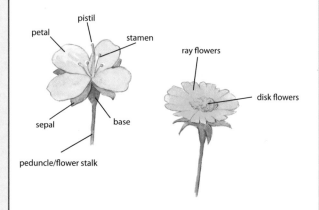

Parts of Leaf

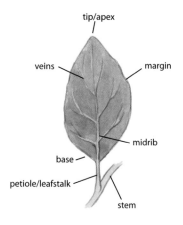

Plant Terms

For the most part, I have chosen to use common terms to describe the plants, although botanists have developed an elaborate language of their own. A few of the scientific terms that I have included in the text have to do with flower parts, leaf shape, margins, and arrangement and are illustrated here.

Leaf Arrangement

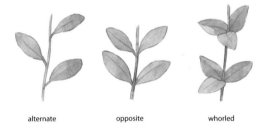

| alternate | opposite | whorled |

Leaf Margins

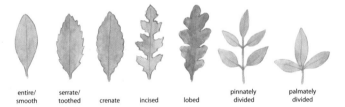

entire/ smooth   serrate/ toothed   crenate   incised   lobed   pinnately divided   palmately divided

Common Leaf Shapes

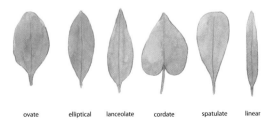

ovate   elliptical   lanceolate   cordate   spatulate   linear

Sea Lettuce, *Ulva lactura*
Chlorophyta (green algae), family Ulvaceae (sea lettuce family)
Alternate name(s): Green laver
Size: 8" across or larger
Range: Coastal regions
Season: Year-round
Habitat: Clings to rocks in tidal zones, piers
Description: Sea lettuce is a sessile, thin, flat, bright green to deep olive-green algae with a lobed and wavy, ragged margin. It may form roundish sheets or longer, thinner blades. It has no stem but attaches directly to the substrate with a disk-shaped holdfast. This delicate algae is extremely thin, being only two cells thick.
Uses: Sea lettuce can be eaten raw as is or chopped up for salads. The dried fronds can be used as a wrap for sushi rolls or crumbled for a salty seasoning in other foods. Also popular added to soups. It is very nutritious, being high in vitamins and minerals, especially iron.

Scouring Rush, *Equisetum hyemale*
Equisetophyta, family Equisetaceae (horsetail family)
Alternate name(s): Horsetail, equisetum
Size: To 3' tall
Range: Throughout the United States
Season: Year-round; produces spores in spring
Habitat: Moist, disturbed areas; wetlands
Description: Scouring rush is one of the last surviving members of this prehistoric group of nonflowering, vascular plants that predates the dinosaurs. Reproducing from spores or from underground rhizomes, it often forms dense colonies. The stems are unbranched, erect, hollow, segmented tubes that are finely ridged longitudinally and impregnated with tiny, silica-containing nodules, giving them a rough, scratchy texture. The leaves are reduced to thin, dark scales that appear at the segments of the stem. At the stem tip grows a cone-shaped cap, called a *strobilus*, that produces and releases the spores.
Uses: The young, emerging sprouts can be boiled and eaten as asparagus or fried. It is known to cause sickness in certain livestock or in humans if eaten in large quantities. Because of the high silica content, scouring rush makes an excellent material for cleaning pots and pans or polishing wooden or metal artifacts.

Bracken Fern, *Pteridium aquilinum*
Polypodiophyta, family Dennstaedtiaceae (bracken fern family)
Size: Up to 6′ tall
Range: Throughout the United States
Season: Year-round but may lose its leaves in colder climates
Habitat: Moist, well-drained soils; can withstand acidic soils
Description: The bracken fern is a perennial, herbaceous plant that is among the most primitive of the vascular plants. It has fronds emerging from a basal rhizome, or rootstock, that can support several fern clumps. Mature fronds are triangular in shape and three times pinnately divided. Leaflets at the base of each frond are quite irregular, whereas those toward the tip become smooth. The underside margins of leaves have small, spore-producing knobs called *sori*.
Uses: The young, developing fronds are known as fiddleheads and can be eaten as asparagus, raw or cooked. Rhizomes are used as a thickening agent in flour or in confections, and they can also be eaten as a vegetable. Bracken fern is best eaten in moderation and cooked because there is evidence that it may contain carcinogens in the raw state.

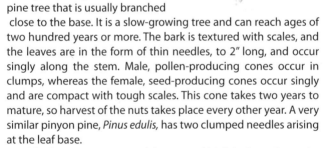

Pinyon Pine, *Pinus monophylla*
Gymnosperms, family Pinaceae
(pine family)
Alternate name(s): One-leaf pinyon
pine, piñon pine
Size: To 35' tall
Range: Southwestern United States
Season: Year-round, cones in summer
Habitat: High desert, mesas, foothills
Description: The pinyon pine is a
woody, relatively small, rounded
pine tree that is usually branched
close to the base. It is a slow-growing tree and can reach ages of
two hundred years or more. The bark is textured with scales, and
the leaves are in the form of thin needles, to 2" long, and occur
singly along the stem. Male, pollen-producing cones occur in
clumps, whereas the female, seed-producing cones occur singly
and are compact with tough scales. This cone takes two years to
mature, so harvest of the nuts takes place every other year. A very
similar pinyon pine, *Pinus edulis,* has two clumped needles arising
at the leaf base.
Uses: The large pine nuts are delicious and high in fat and protein.
Baking or burning of the cones will render the shells easier to
remove. Nuts can then be eaten raw, roasted further, or ground
into a meal to be used in baking. As with most pines, the woody
flesh just inside the bark can be eaten, although it is very tough.
The sap can be used as a chewing gum, as waterproofing for pots,
or as a kind of glue. The wood makes fragrant firewood.

Wapato, *Sagittaria latifolia*
Monocots, family Alismataceae
(water-plantain family)
Alternate name(s): Broad-leaved
arrowhead, tule-potato
Size: To 4' tall, usually smaller
Range: Throughout the
United States
Season: Flowers summer
through early autumn
Habitat: Edges of ponds, streams and lakes, swamps
Description: Wapato is a perennial, aquatic plant that grows fully submerged in water. The roots have lateral runners that terminate in a bulbous tuber that will produce new plants the following season. Leaves arise on a long stalk that rises above the water surface and have the distinctive arrowhead shape with long, backward-projecting lobes but can vary greatly from this shape. Flowering stalks are basal as well, terminating with a spike containing whorls of three white, three-petaled flowers with a globular, greenish center. The seedpods are green balls that turn brown and contain many buoyant seeds.
Uses: The tubers are found underwater in the mud and muck, often some distance from the base of the plant, and can be broken away with a shovel or hoe, whereby they will float to the surface. The largest tubers are collected in the spring or late autumn, when the plant's energy is not focused on the leaves and flowers. They are best peeled and boiled as a potato, or they may be roasted or fried. Young shoots and leaves are also edible, cooked as most greens.

Nut-Grass, *Cyperus esculentus*
Monocots, family Cyperaceae
(sedge family)
Alternate name(s): Chufa, chufa
sedge, yellow nut sedge
Size: To 30" tall
Range: Throughout the United
States
Season: Flowers in summer
Habitat: Mudflats; low, moist fields
Description: Nut-grass is an herbaceous, fibrous, perennial, grasslike
sedge. The root produces a single, erect stem that is three-sided
in cross-section with thin, long, clasping, basal leaves that resemble grass blades. The tiny, greenish flowers are borne on several
umbrella-like clusters (umbels) at an upper node on the stem,
which also sprouts several long, leaflike bracts. The root system
produces segmented rhizomes that terminate in enlarged, roundish tubers.
Uses: The tubers, called tiger nuts, can be used much like a small
potato, steamed or boiled. They are also edible raw, thinly sliced
or shredded in salads. A flavorful flour for baking can be made by
roasting and grinding the tubers. Dark roasted tubers can also be
ground for a coffee substitute. In Spain, a popular drink is made of
the crushed tuber juice with water and sugar.

Bulrush, *Scirpus validus*
Monocots, family Cyperaceae (bulrush family)
Alternate name(s): Tule
Size: To 8' tall
Range: Throughout the United States
Season: Flowers spring through autumn
Habitat: Most wetland areas, fresh or brackish
Description: The bulrush is a tall, perennial, grasslike sedge of wetlands. It forms dense stands, often in the company of cattails, that arise from a spreading, underground rhizome system. Stems are rounded to almost triangular in cross-section, smooth, with a pithy center, and quite thick at the base. There are no real leaves. Loose clusters of tiny flowers form on drooping spikes at the stem's tip and produce spiky, dark brown seed heads.
Uses: The bulrush is a highly versatile plant for food. The young shoots and the soft, inner core of older stems can be eaten raw or cooked. The rootstock can be prepared as potatoes and has a mild sweetness. Seeds are bristly but can be eaten as is or ground into flour for baking. The pollen makes a nutritious addition to other flours. Bulrush also serves an important role as food for wildlife.

Wild Onion, *Allium stellatum*
Monocots, family Liliacea (lily family)
Alternate name(s): Prairie onion, fall glade onion, cliff onion
Size: To 20" tall
Range: Central United States
Season: Flowers summer through autumn
Habitat: Rocky soils, fields
Description: The wild onion is a perennial, herbaceous, native relative of the cultivated onion. Its foliage is sparse, with thin, grass-like, solid leaf blades that arise from a basal bulb. The flower stalk is stiff and erect, arising above the leaves as the leaves begin to die back. The tiny flowers are white to pink to reddish, with a corolla of three petals and three sepals, forming a star shape, with a bright yellow center of stamens. They form a cluster in the form of an umbel. The fruit is a small capsule containing black seeds. All foliage, including the bulb, has a distinctive onion odor.
Uses: The young leaves can be used as a delicious addition to greens in salads or as flavoring in cooked dishes. The bulb can be eaten as the commercial onion: used raw, cooked, roasted, pickled, or used for flavoring.

Wild Leek, *Allium tricoccum*
Monocots, family Liliaceae
(lily family)
Alternate name(s): Ramp
Size: To 20" tall
Range: Midwestern and eastern`
United States
Season: Flowers in summer
Habitat: Moist hardwood forests
Description: The wild leek is an annual, herbaceous relative of the onion that forms spreading clumps as it reproduces vegetatively by the division of its bulb. In early spring it sends up two or three drooping, broadly lanceolate, parallel-veined leaves that are much wider than typical onion leaves and have a reddish midrib near the base. As these die back in summer, an erect flowering stalk grows and produces an umbel of small, white, three-petaled flowers. The seeds formed are small, round, and black and may remain on the stalk throughout the season or into winter.
Uses: Harvesting of wild leek is done by digging up a section of a clump, leaving the rest to reproduce. The bulb is most flavorful in the spring but is edible throughout the year. Remove the outer sheath and use the bulb as an onion for a spicy flavoring or as a vegetable. It can also be pickled. The young leaves, harvested before the plant flowers, are onion-scented and make a good addition to salads or cooked dishes.

Brodiaea, *Brodiaea pulchella* or
Dichelostemma capitatum
Monocots, family Liliaceae (lily family)
Alternate name(s): Fool's onion, wild
hyacinth, blue dicks
Size: To 20" tall
Range: Western United States
Season: Flowers spring through summer
Habitat: Grassy fields, disturbed areas, open woodlands
Description: Brodiaea is a perennial, herbaceous, onion-like plant in
the lily family. From a bulb deep in the ground arise thin, grasslike leaves that are often curled into a tube, especially near the
base. A single flowering stalk terminates with a compact cluster of
six-petaled, pale purple flowers. It can propagate by underground
lateral roots (stolons) that produce new bulbs or by seed.
Uses: Brodiaea has been a very important food in Native American
cultures. The bulbs, which are normally about the size of a large
marble, can be eaten raw, roasted, baked, or boiled. They have
a delicious, mild, nutty flavor. Always collect bulbs that are still
attached to a flower stalk so as not to confuse the plant with the
similar-looking white-flowered death camas.

13

Camus, *Camassia quamash*
Monocots, family Liliaceae (lily family)
Size: To 30" tall
Range: Western United States
Season: Flowers spring through autumn
Habitat: Moist meadows, woodland openings

Description: Camus is a native, perennial, herbaceous member of the lily family that may grow in abundance across western meadows. The leaves are long and grasslike, with pointed tips and parallel venation. They are erect and arise basally from a thick, onion-shaped bulb. A single, unbranched flowering stalk terminates in a spike of pale to deep blue-violet flowers, to about 1.5" in diameter. They have six thin tepals (petals plus sepals), giving the flower a distinct star shape.

Uses: The sugar-rich bulb is the edible part of camus. It can be roasted or boiled as a potato and has a sweet flavor. It was a very important food for Native Americans and early settlers. If the bulb is boiled down, it will yield a sugary syrup. Bulbs are best collected after flowering, but extreme care should be taken not to confuse this plant with the poisonous death camas, which has white flowers but a similar-looking bulb.

Orange Day Lily,

Hemerocallis fulva

Monocots, family Liliaceae (lily family)

Alternate name(s): Tiger day lily

Size: To 4' tall

Range: Throughout the United States except for the Southwest

Season: Flowers in summer

Habitat: Disturbed areas, gardens, roadsides

Description: Natives of eastern Asia, day lilies were brought here as ornamentals but are now present as wild plants, having escaped from gardens. The orange day lily is a perennial, herbaceous, clumping plant that propagates primarily from underground rhizomes. The basal leaves are long, grasslike, and bent longitudinally down the middle as a keel. Small, bractlike leaves appear higher on the stem. The flowering stalks produce several buds that bloom successively, each for only one day (hence the name day lily). The flower is large, showy, and red-orange, with three petals and three somewhat smaller sepals. The base of the flower is an elongated tube, and the fruit is a capsule.

Uses: The day lily is a versatile food, with most of the parts being edible. The flower buds, which taste like beans, and the young shoots can be cooked as vegetables. The flowers can be added to dishes, fresh or dried, and are popular in Asian cuisine. Finally, the underground, bulbous tubers are delicious raw in salads or cooked.

Yucca, *Yucca filamentosa*
Monocots, family Liliaceae
(lily family)
Alternate name(s): Bear-grass,
Adam's needle
Size: Stalk to 10' tall
Range: Southwest and mid-
Atlantic coastal United States
Season: Flowers late spring
through summer
Habitat: Disturbed areas with sandy soils, open woodlands, fields
Description: Yucca is a hardy, evergreen, herbaceous perennial that is native to the eastern United States but is now often used as a garden ornamental. The leaves are basal and form a clumping rosette. They are bluish green, long, and spearlike with a pointed tip, and their margins shred into thin, hairlike, curling threads. A towering flower stalk grows erect and supports many showy flowers on a terminal panicle. Flowers are sweet-scented and pearly white, have a six-petal/sepal corolla, and hang on the stalk like bells. The resulting fruit is a capsule.
Uses: Yucca flower petals make a decorative addition to salads or can be added to soups and cooked dishes. The root can be pounded into a poultice to relieve skin irritation and insect bites or used as a kind of soap. Seed capsules of related species are large and fleshy and make a good cooked vegetable. Native Americans used the fibrous leaves in basket making.

Common Barley, *Hordeum vulgare*
Monocots, family Poaceae (grass family)
Size: To 4' tall
Range: Throughout the United
States
Season: Summer for grain
Habitat: Disturbed areas, road-
sides, pastures
Description: A native of the Middle East, common barley is the same
species as the cultivated variety but now inhabits many wild habitats. It is a tall, erect, annual grass with sparse, clasping, thin, linear
leaves. At the tip of the stem is a spike with a tight cluster of flowers that forms into typically six vertical rows of large grains. The
husk of each grain is tipped with a very long, stiff spine, giving the
cluster the look of a witch's broom.
Uses: Barley has an ancient history of human use and is still
revered today because of its high protein content and large
grain size. The main edible part is the seed, or grain, that ripens
during the summer. It must be removed from the surrounding
husks and chaff by a combination of parching and sifting. Grains
can be eaten cooked in water, used in cereals and baked goods,
or ground into flour. Barley is also an important ingredient in the
production of beer.

Wild Rice, *Zizania aquatica*
Monocots, family Poaceae (grass family)
Alternate name(s): Indian rice,
manoomin
Size: To 10' tall
Range: Midwestern and northeastern
United States
Season: Grains in autumn
Habitat: Lakes, slow-moving rivers,
sloughs
Description: Native to North America,
wild rice is an erect, tall, annual
aquatic grass that forms wide swaths
offshore in water up to four feet
deep. From its underwater root in

the mud, thin, long, lanceolate leaves arise to the surface and produce a floating mat. Eventually, a flowering stalk grows upright
with a delicate, bushy spike of female flowers at the tip and male
flowers just below. The seeds that form are the familiar elongate
kernels encased in a rough husk.
Uses: The rice grains are nutritious and have a delicious, wild, nutty
flavor. They are harvested in the autumn from a boat by knocking
the ripened seed clusters onto a tarp or into a vessel, parching
them, and winnowing the grain from the chaff. They are prepared
by boiling in water as commercial rice. The ground grain makes a
hearty flour that can be used for baking. Care should be taken not
to eat rice where plants are infected with the ergot fungus, which
forms purplish growths and is toxic.

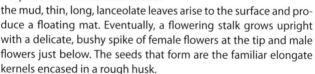

Common Cattail, *Typha latifolia*
Monocots, family Typhaceae (cattail family)
Alternate name(s): Broadleaf cattail
Size: To 8' tall
Range: Throughout the United States
Season: Spring through summer for flowers
Habitat: Marshes, shallow wetlands
Description: Providing habitat and food
for a wide array of animals, the perennial
common cattail grows tall, forming large
stands propagated by creeping, underground rhizomes. Long, linear, pointed
leaves grow along tough, unbranched
stems that emerge from the submerged
root base. A solid spike of greenish, female
(pistillate) flowers forms in the familiar sausage shape. Above this
is a smaller, yellowish clump of male (stamenate) flowers. The
male flowers fall away, and the female flower clump remains and
turns brown.
Uses: The common cattail is a highly useful plant with an ancient
history. The young, emerging shoots can be peeled and eaten
raw or boiled as a vegetable. Before flowers emerge, the green,
bud-filled spikes can be eaten raw or cooked like corn on the
cob. Pollen from the top male flowers can be collected, dried,
and blended with flour for baking. The rootstock is starchy and
can be prepared into a flour by separating out the fibrous tissue
in water. The bulbous nodes on the rhizome can be eaten raw or
cooked. The leaves are useful for weaving, and the fluffy down on
the seeds makes an insulative stuffing.

Green Amaranth, *Amaranthus retroflexus*
Dicots, family Amaranthaceae (pigweed family)
Alternate name(s): Redroot
Size: To 3' tall
Range: Throughout the United States
Season: Flowers spring through summer
Habitat: Disturbed areas, gardens, fields
Description: Green amaranth is one of many species of amaranth that occurs in North America. It is a tall, herbaceous annual with a thick, hairy, branched stem. The leaves are large, lanceolate to ovate, with pinnate venation and smooth margins. Bushy, green flower clusters form in spikes at the apex of the plant, producing small, black seeds in late autumn. The root is thick, branched, and colored rose or pink.
Uses: The leaves of green amaranth are mild in flavor and can be eaten raw in salads or cooked like spinach. The young flower clusters are also good, boiled until tender. The seeds are harvested by collecting ripened flower clusters, then thrashing them when dry. They can be eaten roasted, made into porridge, or ground into flour for baking.

Staghorn Sumac, *Rhus typhina*
Dicots, family Anacardiaceae
(cashew family)

Size: To 30' tall
Range: Northeastern United States
Season: Late summer to autumn
for fruit cluster
Habitat: Fields, disturbed areas, woodland edges
Description: The staghorn sumac is a tall shrub or small tree with sparse, thick branches. The young, growing branches are coated with fine hairs, resembling the velvet of a stag's horn. The alternately arranged leaves grow up to 2' long and are pinnately divided into many lanceolate leaflets with serrate margins. The leafstalks are densely hairy. The characteristic fruiting cluster is cone-shaped and composed of many nonfleshy, hairy, deep rusty-red fruits. The leaves turn a beautiful red in autumn, and the clusters may remain attached to the plant throughout the winter. This plant propagates by seeds or underground rhizomes, and so often it will form closely spaced groups.
Uses: The fruit cluster of staghorn sumac can be used to prepare a refreshing, lemonade-like beverage. Soak the ripened clusters in cold water, strain out the liquid, and add sugar to taste. The young shoots or suckers from stumps can be peeled, cleaned of leaves, and eaten raw. The roots have been used to create a yellow dye.

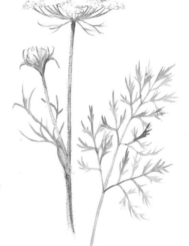

Queen Anne's Lace,

Daucus carota
Dicots, family Apiaceae/Umbelliferae
(carrot family)

Alternate name(s): Wild carrot
Size: To 36" tall
Range: Throughout the United
States
Season: Flowers spring through autumn
Habitat: Disturbed areas, fields, roadsides
Description: Queen Anne's lace is an herbaceous, erect, biennial plant that has a thick taproot and a sturdy stem studded with somewhat coarse, short hairs. The leaves arise alternately on the stem, are based by a thin sheath, and are pinnately divided, fernlike, into delicate segments. The flower clusters appear in flat umbels, about 4" across, at the top of the stem and are based by three-pronged bracts. The flowers are tiny with white petals, sometimes with a reddish flower in the center of the umbel, and resemble delicate lacework. Eventually, the umbel curls up to form a concave, bird's-nest shape.
Uses: The sturdy, white taproot is edible and can be cooked as a carrot. It is best harvested from first-year plants, otherwise it can be quite tough. Be careful not to confuse Queen Anne's lace with the poison hemlock, which has hairless stems, unpleasant scent, and less-divided leaves.

Sweet Fennel,
Foeniculum vulgare
Dicots, family Apiaceae/Umbelliferae
(carrot family)
Alternate name(s): Anise
Size: To 6' tall
Range: Throughout the United States
Season: Flowers spring through autumn
Habitat: Disturbed areas, stream sides
Description: Sweet fennel is a perennial, erect, herbaceous plant introduced from the Mediterranean region, with every part of the plant having the familiar licorice or anise scent. One or several thick stems arise from an enlarged, basal bulb and at nodes produce leaves that are finely dissected with frilly, feathery leaflets. The base of the leaf is a sheathing bract that clasps the stem. Terminally on the stem, or at leaf axils, are compound umbels of minute, yellow flowers. The seeds are flattened, ridged, and oval.
Uses: Seeds of sweet fennel, green or dried, are a popular spice, used to season many ethnic dishes, especially those with fish. They are used even to flavor body products and toothpaste. The basal bulb and young leaves are quite flavorful and may be used raw, cooked, or added to dishes. The stems can be cooked like a kind of celery. A tea with fennel has a soothing effect on the digestive system.

Wild Parsnip, *Pastinaca sativa*
Dicots, family Apiaceae/Umbelliferae
(carrot family)
Size: To 4' tall
Range: Throughout the United States
Season: Flowers spring through
autumn
Habitat: Disturbed areas, roadsides,
sunny open woodlands
Description: Wild parsnip is an introduced, biennial, herbaceous plant that is the same species as the commercially available parsnip. During the first year, it develops a deep taproot and a basal rosette of pinnately divided leaves with leaflets that are ovate to lobed with serrate margins and that grow at an angle to the petiole. During the second year, the deeply grooved, thick flowering stalk grows erect and bears a compound umbel of many tiny, pale yellow flowers.
Uses: The thick, pale taproot, best when harvested late in the first year, can be eaten and prepared as a carrot, and when cooked it is quite sweet. It is commonly used in stews and vegetable dishes for its spicy qualities and may be roasted as well. Chemicals in the plant, in combination with sunlight, can cause irritation to the skin, so caution is advised to avoid the juicy portions from coming into contact with skin. Care should also be taken not to mistake parsnip for the poison hemlock, which it closely resembles.

Common Milkweed,

Asclepias syriaca
Dicots, family Asclepiadaceae
(milkweed family)
Size: To 6' tall
Range: Eastern United States
Season: Flowers in summer
Habitat: Dry fields, disturbed
areas, open woodlands

Description: Common milkweed is an erect, herbaceous, perennial plant native to eastern North America, with fine, soft pubescence on all of its foliage. The stem is usually unbranched and emits a white, fluid latex when cut (hence the common name). The leaves are large, thick, oval to ovate, and arranged opposite on the stem and have very short petioles. The buds and flowers grow in umbel-like clusters from the upper leaf axils. The flowers are small, pale pink or purple, and have a unique shape whereby the petals face backward, and the fleshy center is raised in a crown shape or "beak." The seedpods have a bumpy texture and release many small seeds with fine, cottony hairs, allowing them to float on the breeze.

Uses: The young shoots and flower bud clusters of the common milkweed are delicious boiled as asparagus. The seedpods, before maturation, are soft and edible cooked. Some sources mention the bitterness or even toxicity of this plant, but this may be in part due to confusion of the plant with the toxic dogbane plant. Milkweed is an important food source for monarch butterflies, and the downy hairs on the seeds make an excellent insulation for clothing, used as goose down.

Yarrow, *Achillea millefolium*
Dicots, family Asteraceae/
Compositae (sunflower family)

Size: To 3' tall

Range: Throughout the United States

Season: Flowers in summer

Habitat: Disturbed areas, sunny fields, roadsides

Description: Yarrow is a widespread, herbaceous perennial that is quite hardy and resistant to drought. It begins as a rosette of long, basal leaves that is so highly divided as to be delicate and feather-like. The fuzzy, erect stalk that emerges supports somewhat smaller leaves, arranged alternately, and terminates in flat umbels of white flowers. These flowers are composite, with (usually) five ray flowers surrounding the tiny, disk flowers. Dried flower stalks may persist through the winter.

Uses: Yarrow has a long history as a medicine, as a topical antiseptic remedy for cuts and bruises, or as a tea made from the leaves and/or flowers that induces sweating and aids digestion. The young, tender leaves have been used as a cooked green or as a seasoning in soups and cooked dishes. Caution is advised due to chemicals in yarrow that can cause skin irritation with extensive handling and due to its close resemblance to the toxic poison hemlock plant.

Great Burdock, *Arctium rappa*
Dicots, family Asteraceae/Compositae
(sunflower family)

Size: To 6' tall
Range: Northeastern United States
Season: Flowers in summer
Habitat: Disturbed areas

Description: Great burdock is a very large, herbaceous biennial introduced from the Old World. In its first year, it produces basal leaves and a strong taproot. In the second year, it grows tall, bushy stems with large (up to 12" long), heart-shaped or ovate leaves with a fine, gray, downy coating on the underside. Atop the stems arise globelike clusters of hooked, green bracts that support many purple, tubelike flowers. When dry, this cluster is a prickly burr that will clasp to clothing and fur.

Uses: The young, tender leaves, as well as the inner part of the stems, can be eaten raw in small quantities alone or added to salads. They have a bitter flavor that can be reduced by boiling in several changes of water. The long, thin taproot can also be eaten after removing the tough outer rind and boiling.

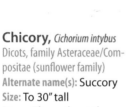

Chicory, *Cichorium intybus*
Dicots, family Asteraceae/Compositae (sunflower family)
Alternate name(s): Succory
Size: To 30" tall
Range: Throughout the
United States
Season: Flowers in summer
Habitat: Disturbed areas, gardens, roadsides
Description: Chicory is a perennial, herbaceous plant introduced from Europe with a basal rosette of deeply incised, dandelion-like leaves with toothed margins. An erect, angular stalk arises from this rosette, bearing several square-tipped and ragged composite flowers that occur along the length of the stem. They are bright lavender blue but also may be whitish or pink. The flower is capable of closing in intense sunlight or in the evening.
Uses: The root can be dried and roasted, then ground and used to brew a coffee-like beverage. Indeed, it is added to coffee as a tradition in southern Cajun cultures. The young, tender leaves and stalks are a bitter green and can be eaten raw or boiled as a spinach-type dish. Chicory is the same plant that can be cultivated as endive.

Bull Thistle, *Cirsium vulgare*
Dicots, family Asteraceae/Compositae
(sunflower family)
Size: To 6′ tall
Range: Throughout the United
States
Season: Flowers in summer
Habitat: Disturbed areas, sunny
fields, roadsides
Description: Bull thistle is an erect, herbaceous biennial that produces a basal rosette of deeply incised leaves in the first year and
tall stalks in the second year. The stems are ribbed vertically with
thin, sharp, prickly "wings." Upper leaves attach directly to the
stem and are divided along their length into sharp, pointed lobes
with spines along the margin. The inflorescence is based by an
urn-shaped clump of bracts with yellow-tipped spines and consists of pink to purple ray flowers, reminiscent of a shaving brush.
Uses: The imposing look of bull thistle belies its versatile use for
food. The roots and shoots can be boiled and eaten as a vegetable. The tender, young leaves can be eaten raw as greens,
and the young stems can be peeled and cooked as asparagus.
Older leaves become bitter, but boiling in two changes of water
will render them palatable. Thistles are relatives of the artichoke,
and thistle heads can be prepared as such, eating the tender
inner part.

Common Sunflower,
Helianthus annuus
Dicots, family Asteraceae/
Compositae (sunflower family)
Size: To 10' tall
Range: Throughout the
United States
Season: Flowers summer
through autumn
Habitat: Disturbed areas,
fields with full sun

Description: The common sunflower is an erect, herbaceous, annual plant native to North America. The stems are thick and well-branched and have a coarse, hairy texture. The leaves are large, alternate on long petioles, ovate to cordate, and have serrate margins. The large flower heads arise on stalks from the leaf axils and are composite, having outer (ray) flowers that are yellow and inner (disk) flowers that are brown. The disk flowers mature into the seeds, which may remain on the stalk through winter, becoming an important food source for birds.

Uses: The seeds of the sunflower are an incredibly versatile food, and they are very high in protein and vitamins. They can be used in much the same way as cultivated sunflower seeds, yet they are much smaller. To harvest the seeds, knock them out of the dried flower heads and roast or parch to more easily separate the kernels from the hulls. Eat as is, in cereals, in cooking, or ground for flour. Boiling the mashed seeds will yield a light cooking oil. Also, the flower buds can be eaten, boiled as a vegetable.

Jerusalem Artichoke,
Helianthus tuberosus
Dicots, family Asteraceae/Compositae
(sunflower family)
Alternate name(s): Sunchoke,
sunroot
Size: To 9′ tall
Range: Eastern United States
Season: Flowers summer through autumn
Habitat: Disturbed areas, roadsides
Description: The Jerusalem artichoke is in the same genus as the common sunflower, is a native of eastern North America, and has been cultivated there for centuries. It is a perennial, erect, herbaceous, well-branched sunflower with coarse, hairy foliage. The leaves begin opposite in the young plant and become alternate higher up the stem. They are elliptic to lanceolate in shape and have serrate margins. The large, composite flowers form from the leaf axils or terminally and have yellow ray flowers and dark yellow disk flowers. The plant can propagate vegetatively by means of enlarged tubers found at the tips of underground, spreading rhizomes.
Uses: The tubers are the primary food source from this plant and are best collected in the nonflowering season when the tuber stores the most carbohydrate and nutrients. They can be prepared much like a potato, peeled or not, by steaming or boiling or frying as french fries. They can also be eaten raw, finely sliced or grated in salads. Some people develop stomach upset from the sweet-tasting chemical, inulin, in the flesh.

Cat's Ear, *Hypochaeris radicata*
Dicots, family Asteraceae/
Compositae (sunflower family)
Alternate name(s): False dandelion,
flatweed
Size: To 30" tall
Range: Throughout the United States
Season: Flowers spring through autumn
Habitat: Disturbed areas, lawns, roadsides
Description: Cat's ear is a perennial, herbaceous, introduced plant that bears a strong resemblance to the dandelion. From a deep taproot, it forms a dense, low-lying rosette of basal leaves that can be virtually flat or somewhat bushy, depending on conditions. The leaves are elliptical with incised lobes that are more rounded than those of a dandelion and are hairy on both the upper and lower surface (like a cat's ear). The flowering stalk is solid, erect and branching and terminates with a small, yellow composite flower. The seed head is a puffy globe, like that of a dandelion but smaller and scruffier.
Uses: The young, tender leaves have a mild, bitter flavor and are good raw mixed into salads or cooked as greens. The flowers are edible and decorative in dishes. The early stalks, just as the flower buds are forming, can be prepared like asparagus.

Nipplewort, *Lapsana communis*
Dicots, family Asteraceae/Compositae
(sunflower family)
Alternate name(s): Dockcress
Size: To 3' tall
Range: Throughout most of the
United States
Season: Flowers spring through autumn
Habitat: Disturbed areas, gardens
Description: Nipplewort is an introduced, herbaceous, annual or
biennial plant, bushy below with sparse foliage above, with a
stout taproot. It begins with a basal rosette of thin, soft, hairy,
dissected leaves that ends with the largest, triangular to ovate
lobe. Erect, hollow, and round stems grow from this rosette and
produce leaves that are less dissected than those near the base,
becoming entire and pointed higher up the stem. The upper
stems have few leaves and produce loose clusters of yellow, composite flowers with toothed ray flowers. Some say that the closed
flower buds resemble nipples and that this resemblance is the
origin of its name.
Uses: The young, tender leaves are edible as a green in salads or as
a boiled potherb. Avoid the older leaves because they are quite
fibrous and bitter. Early, fast-growing stems are edible cooked like
asparagus.

Sow Thistle, *Sonchus oleraceus*
Dicots, family Asteraceae/Compositae
(sunflower family)

Alternate name(s): Smooth sow
thistle

Size: To 8′ tall

Range: Throughout the United
States

Season: Flowers in summer

Habitat: Disturbed areas,
gardens, roadsides

Description: Sow thistle is a tall,
erect, herbaceous annual, introduced from Europe, with large,
prickly edged leaves but smoother and less jagged than its cousin,
the spiny sow thistle. The surface of the leaves is smooth, without
hairs like other sow thistles. The leaves are long, dark green, and
deeply incised with a spiny margin and a thick central vein. They
lack a petiole and instead clasp around the stem at their base. The
stem oozes a white latex when cut. The flowers arise in clumps
of several buds—resembling small dandelions—and form into
small, puffy seed heads.

Uses: Leaves of sow thistle can be eaten raw in salads; young
leaves are best because leaves become bitter and fibrous with
age. Cooking will reduce the bitterness. The stalks can be boiled
and eaten as a vegetable—again, younger, fast-growing stalks
are more tender and less bitter. The early flower buds can also be
eaten, and the young taproots can be cooked like potatoes.

Dandelion, *Taraxacum officinale*
Dicots, family Asteraceae/
Compositae (sunflower family)
Alternate name(s): Dent-de-lion
Size: To 12" tall
Range: Throughout the
United States
Season: Flowers spring through summer
Habitat: Disturbed areas, lawns, roadsides
Description: The bane of those who prefer a pristine lawn, the dandelion is a tenacious, perennial plant that is also a terrific food source. Its name derives from the French word *dent,* meaning "tooth," and *lion,* referring to the jagged margin of the leaf, apparently resembling the tooth of a lion. The deeply incised, long leaves arise from a basal rosette, from which also emerges an unbranched flowering stalk terminating in a bright yellow, composite flower with downward-pointing, green bracts. Soon, the familiar seed head with numerous white, delicate filaments forms. Stems are hollow and emit a milky substance when cut, and there is a long, thick taproot.
Uses: The leaves can be eaten raw in salads but are best when young because they develop intense bitterness with age. Steaming or boiling the leaves renders them more tender and palatable. The flower buds are also edible when cooked as a vegetable. The taproots can be dried and roasted, then ground to be used as a coffee substitute.

Salsify, *Tragopogon porrifolius*
Dicots, family Asteraceae/
Compositae (sunflower family)
Alternate name(s): Oyster plant,
goatsbeard
Size: To 4' tall
Range: Throughout most of the United States except for south-eastern states
Season: Flowers spring through summer
Habitat: Disturbed areas, fields, roadsides
Description: Salsify is an erect, herbaceous plant, introduced from Europe, whose stem and root emit milky latex when cut. Along the sturdy, round stems are long, thin, grasslike leaves that clasp and are continuous with the stem and are arranged alternately. The apex of each stem produces a purplish composite flower with pointed green bracts. The resulting seed head is a globe of delicate, lacy seed structures, like a giant dandelion puffball.
Uses: The thick, tough taproot of salsify can be boiled until tender and eaten as a root vegetable. It has a sweet taste reminiscent of oysters. The young shoots and leaves are also edible and can be prepared like cooked greens. Salsify is cultivated commercially for the root.

Coltsfoot, *Tussilago farfara*
Dicots, family Asteraceae/
Compositae (sunflower family)
Size: To 16" tall
Range: Northeastern United States
Season: Flowers in spring
Habitat: Roadsides, disturbed areas
Description: Coltsfoot is a perennial, nonnative, herbaceous plant that often forms clusters by means of a network of underground rhizomes. It is unusual in that it produces a leafless flowering stalk in the spring before any leaves appear. The stem is thick and covered by reddish, sheathing bracts or scales. A bright yellow composite flower, with somewhat stiff outer ray flowers, blooms at the tip of each stalk, maturing into a dandelion-like, fluffy seed head. The large, heart-shaped leaves (looking roughly like a cross-section of a colt's foot) emerge as the flowers die away, forming a low-lying clump of foliage.
Uses: A tea can be made out of the leaves. The tea has a soothing effect on the respiratory system and reduces coughing. Candy is made from an extract of the leaves cooked with sugar as a kind of cough drop. Burning the leaves and crumbling them provides a saltlike seasoning.

Wild Grape, *Vitus* sp.
Dicots, family Berberidaceae
(barberry family)
Size: Vines to 50' or longer
Range: Throughout the United States
Season: Flowers in summer, fruit into autumn
Habitat: Sunny riparian areas, disturbed areas, roadsides, forest edges
Description: Numerous species of wild grape grow across the United
States, share the same characteristics, and can be used similarly.
They are perennial and develop a woody, peeling stalk that pro-
duces fresh vegetation each year. The stems creep and entwine
surrounding trees and shrubs, taking hold with curling, fork-
tipped tendrils. The leaves are fairly large, arranged alternately,
and are heart-shaped or variably lobed, with dentate margins.
Small, greenish flowers arise in clusters and produce tiny, green
fruits that grow and ripen to small grapes that can range in color
from purple to black to brownish yellow.
Uses: Wild grapes eaten right off the vine can vary from quite sour
to sweet, depending on the state of ripeness. They can be made
into a strong, tart juice, mixed in with other juices, or cooked into
jelly that is much more flavorful than commercial grape jellies.
They can also be used to make wine. The young, tender leaves are
edible raw or boiled.

American Hazelnut,

Corylus americana
Dicots, family Betulaceae
(birch family)

Alternate name(s): Filbert

Size: To 10' tall

Range: Eastern United States

Season: Flowers in summer, nuts in autumn

Habitat: Mixed woodlands, stream sides, wet areas. Can survive in low-light areas

Description: The American hazelnut is a large, fast-growing, well-branched, deciduous shrub that can propagate by underground rhizomes, so it often forms dense thickets. Its smaller branches and petioles are covered in stiff hairs. Leaves are ovalate to heart-shaped, to 4" long, with pointed tips and margins that are double-serrated (have sets of small teeth between larger teeth). The leaves turn a beautiful reddish color in the autumn. Male flowers are yellow-green and grow in drooping catkins, whereas the clusters of female flowers form an oval nut encased in an open-ended, tube-shaped, rough, and ragged husk.

Uses: The nuts are delicious raw or roasted after being removed from the husk. The roasted nuts can also be made into flour for baking and are popular as a candy by dipping them in syrup. Wood from the thick stems and roots is valued in woodworking. The nuts and flowering stalks are an important food source for wildlife, and the dense growth of hazelnut provides shelter.

Comfrey, *Symphytum officinale*
Dicots, family Boraginaceae
(borage family)
Alternate name(s): Boneset, knitbone
Size: To 4' tall
Range: Scattered regions throughout the United States
Season: Flowers through summer
Habitat: Meadows, stream sides
Description: Comfrey is a perennial, herbaceous plant introduced from Europe that has become naturalized over much of North America. It is gangly and fast-growing and forms clumps of foliage. The erect stem is winged with a thin edge and bears leaves in an alternate arrangement. The leaves are hairy, oval to lanceolate, with pointed tips and smooth margins. The flowers arise terminally or in leaf axils, forming loose clusters that sometimes droop into a coil at the tip of the stalk and are flanked by a pair of upright leaves. The flowers have five petals, are purplish, and hang like bells.
Uses: Comfrey has a history of healing properties. The young, tender leaves are edible cooked as greens or boiled in two changes of water to reduce bitterness. A tea, known to soothe digestive disorders, can be made with the leaves or with dried and powdered roots. A poultice of the roots or leaves is used to reduce swelling and soothe bruises, burns, and muscle pain.

Wintercress, *Barbarea vulgaris*
Dicots, family Brassicaceae/Cruciferae
(mustard family)

Size: To 2' tall

Range: Most of the United States except
the warmest, southern zones

Season: Flowers in the spring

Habitat: Disturbed soils with sufficient moisture

Description: Wintercress is an herbaceous, annual or two- or three-year perennial, capable of overwintering even in very cold climates. The larger leaves are dark green overall, crisp, and shiny. The plant begins as a basal rosette of stalked leaves with rounded lobes, ending with the largest lobe. The erect stem is deeply ridged, and the leaves emerge alternately and clasp the stem. They are rounded to lanceolate with uneven margins. Yellow-green buds form in clusters and produce tiny, bright yellow, four-petaled flowers. The seedpods are long and narrow, with a short tip, or "beak."

Uses: The tender, young leaves, before flowering begins, are best. They can be eaten raw or boiled to reduce bitterness. The upper stem with bud clusters can be cooked like broccoli. The flower petals can be steeped to make a bitter tea, known to be a diuretic.

41

Field Mustard, *Brassica rapa* or
Brassica campestris
Dicots, family Brassicaceae/Cruciferae
(mustard family)
Alternate name(s): Rape, wild turnip
Size: To 28" tall
Range: Throughout the United States
Season: Flowers spring through summer
Habitat: Disturbed areas, gardens,
fields, roadsides

Description: Field mustard was introduced from southern Europe and makes beautiful fields of yellow in the spring. It grows as a fast-growing annual or a biennial that sprouts in the autumn and forms a cluster of basal leaves that develops the following spring. Its foliage is covered with a thin, white coating. The leaves are alternate on the stem. Lower leaves are deeply incised with a jagged margin, whereas upper leaves are elongate with lobes at the base that clasp the stem. The flowers are small, four-petaled, and yellow and appear in clusters. They produce the familiar elongate, upward-facing seedpods with a terminal, pointed "beak." The genus *Brassica* includes many crop plants, including broccoli, cauliflower, turnips, kohlrabi, cabbage, kale, and rapeseed.

Uses: Small amounts of the young, raw leaves are good in salads, although the flavor is quite bitter. Boiling in water will render the leaves tender and less bitter. The seedpods, when young, are edible as well. Young, developing flower bud clusters may be eaten raw or cooked like miniature broccoli. The seeds can be used as a spice or prepared as the standard mustard condiment.

Sea Rocket, *Cakile edentula*
Dicots, family Brassicaceae/
Cruciferae (mustard family)
Alternate name(s): Cakile
Size: To 20" tall
Range: Coastal western and eastern United States
Season: Flowers summer through early autumn
Habitat: Sandy, coastal beaches
Description: Sea rocket is an introduced, annual, low-growing, suc-
culent plant of the mustard family that grows in coastal regions.
The leaves are fleshy and grow alternately on the well-branched
stems. They are oblong to lanceolate and thick; have an irregular,
loosely toothed or lobed margin; and taper down to the stem. The
flowers grow terminally on the stems in a loose spike; are small,
four-petaled, white to pale purple; and mature into two-parted
seedpods with a larger oblong pod atop a smaller one.
Uses: The tender leaves of sea rocket can be eaten raw in salads
or cooked as a potherb. They have a strong, peppery taste. Most
other plant parts, including the buds, early seedpods, and stems,
are edible cooked as an accompaniment to other dishes.

43

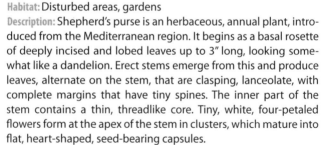

Shepherd's Purse,

Capsella bursa-pastoris
Dicots, family Brassicaceae/Cruciferae
(mustard family)

Size: To 20" tall
Range: Throughout the United States
Season: Flowers in the spring
Habitat: Disturbed areas, gardens
Description: Shepherd's purse is an herbaceous, annual plant, introduced from the Mediterranean region. It begins as a basal rosette of deeply incised and lobed leaves up to 3" long, looking somewhat like a dandelion. Erect stems emerge from this and produce leaves, alternate on the stem, that are clasping, lanceolate, with complete margins that have tiny spines. The inner part of the stem contains a thin, threadlike core. Tiny, white, four-petaled flowers form at the apex of the stem in clusters, which mature into flat, heart-shaped, seed-bearing capsules.
Uses: The young leaves, before flowering begins, can be eaten raw as a salad. They become tough and bitter in mature plants, but simmering them in water will render them more palatable. The seeds, taken from the capsules and dried, can be used whole or ground for a nice, peppery spice.

Watercress, *Nasturtium officinale*
Dicots, family Brassicaceae/Cruciferae
(mustard family)

Size: Stems to 20" long

Range: Throughout the United States

Season: Flowers spring through autumn

Habitat: Streams, wetlands with circulating water, stream banks

Description: Watercress is an aquatic, low-lying, herbaceous, perennial plant related to mustard and cabbage. It has hollow stems and a creeping nature, allowing it to float on the water's surface and form dense mats, with some stems that grow erect. The leaves are alternately arranged and pinnately divided into oval or lanceolate, succulent leaflets. The white, four-petaled flowers grow in clusters terminally on the stems and produce thin, sausage-shaped seedpods (siliques) typical of the mustard family that mature beneath the continually flowering tip. Nodes along the stems form new roots and allow the plant to spread vegetatively.

Uses: The young, tender leaves and stems are excellent greens, eaten alone or mixed with other greens in salads. They have a strong, crisp, spicy taste like pepper. The upper portions of the plant are best. A prized food since ancient times, watercress is filled with nutrients and has a number of health benefits. Due to the plant's ability to absorb quantities of minerals from the water, it is advised to avoid harvesting in areas that may be polluted.

Prickly Pear Cactus,
Opuntia basilaris
Dicots, family Cactacea (cactus family)
Alternate name(s): Beavertail
cactus, tuna, nopales
Size: Sprawling, to 20" tall
Range: Southwestern United States
Season: Pads in spring, fruit in autumn
Habitat: Deserts
Description: As a group, the cacti are native only to the Western Hemisphere. The prickly pear cactus is among many species of *Opuntia* (one of which, *O. humifusa,* is common in eastern states) that can be used similarly. The fleshy, succulent stem segments are flattened into lobes, or "pads," with joints in between. The surface is dotted with both long, thick spines and short, barbed spines that are easily broken and stick into the skin with careless handling. The flowers are showy, many-petaled, and colored pink to rose. The ripened fruit is a reddish or purple, fleshy knob at the flower base. This cactus can reproduce vegetatively, and so it often forms dense clusters.
Uses: To avoid the painful prickles, always wear gloves when harvesting the prickly pear cactus. The young, growing pads are edible peeled and cooked or used in cooking as a thickening agent. The fleshy fruit can be eaten raw, taking care to avoid the spines on the outer rind, or made into jellies or juice. The flower buds are edible and can be roasted. Related to the chollas, which are now in a separate genus, the prickly pear provides excellent habitat and food for all manner of desert-dwelling birds, mammals, reptiles, and insects.

Chickweed, *Stellaria media*
Dicots, family Caryophyllaceae
(pink family)

Alternate name(s): Common chickweed, starwort

Size: To 12" tall

Range: Throughout the United States

Season: Early spring or late autumn; dies off if too hot. Grows through the winter in mild climates

Habitat: Disturbed areas with rich, moist soil

Description: Introduced from Europe, chickweed is a common, herbaceous annual. It is low-growing and creeps across the ground with thin, spindly stems that have a narrow, single line of longitudinal hairs. The leaves are opposite on short petioles, bright green, usually less than 1" long, and oval to elliptic in shape, with pointed tips and smooth margins. The flowers are tiny, with five white petals that are deeply cleft, giving the look of ten separate petals.

Uses: Chickweed is high in potassium, iron, and antioxidants. The leaves and upper stem tips, including the buds and flowers, can be eaten raw in salads or cooked like spinach. They have a pleasant, mild, nonbitter taste. Plant parts lower on the stalk have a tougher, stringy texture and less pleasant taste.

Wild Spinach,

Chenopodium album

Dicots, family Chenopodiaceae (goosefoot family)

Alternate name(s): Lamb's quarters, pigweed, goosefoot

Size: To 4' tall

Range: Throughout the United States

Season: Flowers in summer

Habitat: Disturbed areas, gardens

Description: Introduced from Europe, wild spinach is a weedy, annual, herbaceous plant with an erect stature and a long tap-root. The leaves are alternate and roundish to pointed, with serrate margins. Clusters of buds produce tiny, nondescript, greenish flowers, which in turn produce tiny, black seeds. The entire surface, especially the shoots and young leaves, is covered with a mealy, waxy substance.

Uses: A delicious and highly nutritious wild green, wild spinach is rich in vitamins and minerals, especially potassium. The leaves have a pleasant texture and mild flavor and can be eaten raw in salads or cooked as spinach. The seeds ripen in late autumn and can be made into a cooked cereal, ground into flour for baking, or roasted. The flower bud clusters are also edible cooked or raw. Native Americans have used the dried and ground roots as a kind of soap.

Pickleweed, *Salicornia europaea*
Dicots, family Chenopodiaceae (goosefoot family)
Alternate name(s): Slender glasswort
Size: To 15" tall
Range: Scattered regions throughout the
United States
Season: Blooms in autumn
Habitat: Coastal or brackish wetlands, alkaline sinks
Description: The pickleweed described here is one of many species known as glassworts or pickleweeds. It is an herbaceous, annual, succulent plant of salty habitats. Bushy or erect in stature, it lacks true leaves and instead forms fleshy, segmented, scaled sections on the stem and branches. The flowers are inconspicuous, dwelling in the axils of branches and between the stem segments. The tissues in the plant readily absorb and store sodium from its favored soil and water environments. Pickleweed turns reddish in the late autumn and often forms dense stands.
Uses: The segmented stems can be eaten raw, chopped in salads, cooked as a potherb, or added to seafood dishes. They have a distinct, salty flavor. The stems are also popular pickled in vinegar and spices. Native cultures used the seeds, dried and ground, as a flour for baking. The burned plant makes an ash high in soda content and has been used in the glass-making process, hence the common name glasswort.

Bunchberry,

Cornus canadensis
Dicots, family Cornaceae
(dogwood family)

Alternate name(s): Miner's dogwood, dwarf cornel
Size: To 8" tall
Range: Northeastern United States, Rocky Mountains
Season: Flowers early summer, fruit late summer through autumn
Habitat: Moist, open woodlands of cooler climates
Description: Bunchberry is a perennial, small, slow-growing herbaceous kind of dogwood that sometimes forms extensive stands on the forest floor. It can reproduce vegetatively by means of underground rhizomes that send up shoots of new plants. The stems are short and thin and support oppositely arranged or whorls of dark green, ovate, pointed leaves. They have smooth margins and distinctive parallel venation. The flower is a showy combination to four white, petal-like leaves with a cluster of tiny, greenish flowers in the center. The berries are borne in a compact bunch (hence the common name), begin green, and mature to bright red.
Uses: The berries can be eaten raw when fully ripe. They have a very subtle, slightly sweet flavor. They dry well for later munching or can be added to cereals and baked goods. A nice sauce, syrup, or jelly can be made by boiling the berries with water and sugar. Bunchberries are also an important food source for wildlife.

Live-Forever, *Sedum purpureum*
Dicots, family Crassulaceae
(stonecrop family)
Alternate name(s): Orpine
Size: To 24" tall
Range: Midwestern and eastern
United States
Season: Flowers in summer
Habitat: Disturbed areas, roadsides, open woodlands
Description: Live-forever is a succulent, perennial, erect member of the stonecrop family. The thick, pithy stem produces leaves alternately or in whorls. The leaves are large, fleshy, light green, and ovate to spoon-shaped and have a bluntly serrate margin. The small flowers are pale pink to reddish purple, five-petaled, star-shaped, and grouped terminally on the stem in a domed cluster. The root mass is a tangled clump of carrot-shaped tubers.
Uses: The younger, tender leaves of live-forever are edible raw in salads, having a sour or peppery flavor, or can be cooked as greens. The tubers, separated and cleaned, can be pickled or boiled as a potato. The common name live-forever comes from the plant's ability to propagate itself vegetatively from cut pieces of the root or stem segments and from its hardy nature.

American Persimmon,

Diospyros virginiana
Dicots, family Ebenaceae
(ebony family)

Alternate name(s): Eastern
persimmon, simmon, possomwood

Size: To 60' tall or more

Range: Middle and eastern United States

Season: Flowers spring through summer, fruit in late autumn

Habitat: Dry, open woodlands; fields

Description: American persimmon is a woody, deciduous tree with a well-branched trunk, with sometimes-drooping branches and a rounded crown. Older bark is very dark (almost black) and cracked into rectangular blocks. The leaves are alternate, oval with pointed tips, and have a smooth margin. They are dark, shiny green above and paler below, with a short petiole. The flowers are divided between male and female. The more-conspicuous female (staminate) flowers are small, creamy white, fleshy, solitary, four-petaled, and shaped like little bells. The resulting fruit is borne on a short stalk, round and fleshy, and colored orange with a pale bloom. The leaves turn a beautiful yellow-orange to red color in the autumn.

Uses: The unripe fruit contains tannins, which are responsible for a powerful, astringent taste, but when ripe and soft they are delicious and sweet, with a flavor something like dates. They are edible raw (avoiding the seeds) or can be used in baking sweet breads, puddings, sauces, or jams. The leaves are also useful steeped for tea.

Kinnikinik, *Arctostaphylos uva-ursi*
Dicots, family Ericaceae (heath family)
Alternate name(s): Bearberry
Size: To 18" tall
Range: Most of United States except for the southeast
Season: Blooms in summer, fruit in autumn
Habitat: Rocky, sandy soils; foothills
Description: Kinnikinik is a perennial, native, evergreen, shrubby, trailing plant closely related to manzanita. It grows close to the ground and develops woody stems with reddish-brown, peeling bark. New growth comes from sprouts on the main stems, is often hairy, and supports small, spoon-shaped, thick, leathery leaves with smooth margins. Small, urn-shaped, pale pink flowers are borne in small, drooping clusters that contain a few to over a dozen flowers. The berries are firm, round, bright cranberry red and have a star-shaped flaring tip.
Uses: The ripe berries can be eaten raw but are quite bitter and astringent. They are best cooked down as a sauce with water and sugar. The leaves have been used by Native Americans as a component of smoking mixtures.

Salal, *Gaultheria shallon*
Dicots, family Ericaceae
(heath family)

Alternate name(s): Shallon

Size: To 5' tall

Range: Western United States

Season: Flowers spring through summer

Habitat: Acidic soils of coniferous forests or woodlands with brush; coastal regions

Description: Salal is a native, shrubby, evergreen, perennial relative of manzanita and blueberry that forms a dense, spreading mass. The stems are often reddish. The thick, leathery, dark green leaves are up to 4" long, ovate, with pointed tips and finely serrate margins. The flowers are loosely clustered on terminal stalks and are small, urn-shaped, pale pink or white, with a sticky base. The fruits are plump and dark blue-purple and have a depressed navel at their tips.

Uses: Salal berries are somewhat sweet, like huckleberries, and can be eaten raw or used in cooking. They are especially delicious made into jams, jellies, and pies. Native Americans often dried the berries and made them into cakes or stored them for winter months. A tea of the leaves is known to relieve digestive disorders. The salal plant is an important food source for wildlife as well.

Lowbush Blueberry,

Vaccinium angustifolium
Dicots, family Ericaceae (heath family)
Size: To 18" tall
Range: Northeastern and mid-western United States
Season: Flowers spring through summer, fruit summer through autumn
Habitat: Acidic soils in woodlands and meadows
Description: The lowbush blueberry is one of many closely related and similar-looking native plants referred to as blueberries, bilberries, cranberries, and huckleberries. It is a shrubby, low-growing perennial with leaves that grow alternate on the stem. The leaves are shiny and ovate to lanceolate and turn reddish or purplish in the autumn. The flowers are small, white, and look like little hanging bells. The berries begin whitish or pale green and then achieve their dark blue-purple color. They are plump and round, with a flared, star-shaped tip.
Uses: The berries of the lowbush blueberry are delicious eaten right off the plant and are more intense in flavor than the commercial varieties. To harvest large quantities, place a cloth or tarp under the plant and shake the branches. The ripe berries will fall off readily. Berries can be dried and used later or added to baked goods like muffins, pancakes, or pies. They also make an excellent jam or jelly.

Acacia, *Acacia greggii*
Dicots, family Fabacea/Leguminosae
(pea family)
Alternate name(s): Catclaw
Size: To 15' tall
Range: Southwestern United States
Season: Flowers in spring, pods in
the autumn
Habitat: Arroyos and dry stream beds of deserts, arid woodlands, and scrub
Description: Acacia is a deciduous, perennial, well-branched shrub or small tree. Its most striking feature is the branches, which are lined at intervals with long, arching horns that resemble a cat's claw, giving it its alternate name, catclaw. The leaves are twice pinnately compound, with small, oval or spatulate, grayish-green leaflets. The fragrant, tiny, pale yellow or creamy flowers are borne on loose, cylindrical catkins and mature into large, reddish-brown pods, like peas, that contain the shiny, brown seeds. The pods often curve when dry and may remain on the plant throughout winter.
Uses: The pods can be eaten raw or dried and ground into flour for baking. When green, the seeds also can be eaten raw or, when dried, cooked in dishes as a type of bean. Acacia provides important habitat for desert-dwelling animals, and bees take the nectar to make excellent honey.

Alfalfa, *Medicago sativa*
Dicots, family Fabacea/Leguminosae
(pea family)
Alternate name(s): Lucerne
Size: To 30" tall
Range: Most of the United States
except southeastern states
Season: Flowers spring through autumn
Habitat: Fields, roadsides
Description: Alfalfa is an introduced, herbaceous perennial that is the familiar cultivated crop that is made into hay for animal food but that now grows wild in many regions. It is bushy or sprawling and creates a tough root crown that sprouts new stems each year. The leaves are fairly small and trifoliate and have ovate leaflets that resemble clover. The flowers are purplish blue, occur in rounded spikes, and produce coiled seedpods.
Uses: High in protein and vitamins, alfalfa leaves can be eaten raw, mixed into salads, or boiled as a green. The leaves can also be steeped in hot water for tea. Seeds can be ground to make flour for baking or sprouted in jars for alfalfa sprouts and added to salads or sandwiches. Like most legumes, alfalfa has nodules on its roots that have the ability to fix nitrogen into a form that can be assimilated by it and other plants. Alfalfa flowers are important for bees and the production of honey.

Eastern Chinquapin,

Castanea pumila
Dicots, family Fagaceae
(beech family)
Alternate name(s): Allegheny
chinquapin, dwarf chestnut
Size: To 20' tall
Range: Eastern and southern United States
Season: Flowers in summer, nuts in autumn
Habitat: Arid, sunny uplands on sandy soils
Description: The eastern chinquapin is a relative of the American chestnut but smaller and often more of a bushy shrub than a tree in form. The trunk is well-branched, with grayish, furrowed bark. The leaves are alternate on the stems and ovate with pointed tips and have serrate margins. Venation is fairly straight and crisp, and there are fine white hairs on the underside. Male flowers are yellow and borne in long spikes, whereas the female flowers form a bristly, spherical husk, smaller than a chestnut, that contains a single, smooth, brownish nut.
Uses: The nuts are delicious, removed from the husk and roasted or eaten raw. Roasted nuts can be ground into flour for baking. A popular candy can be made by coating the nuts with syrup or sugar. Also, the leaves can be steeped to make a tea for treatment of colds and flu.

White Oak, *Quercus alba*
Dicots, family Fagaceae (beech family)
Size: To 80' tall
Range: Eastern United States
Season: Acorns in autumn
Habitat: Grows in a wide range of habitats
Description: As a group, the oaks are long-living deciduous trees known for their choice hardwood and the production of acorns. The white oak is a native to eastern North America with a wide canopy and thick, lateral limbs. The trunk can be quite massive, with grayish, cracked, or scaly bark. Leaves are alternate on the stems, somewhat oval or oblong, with several broad lobes and a smooth margin. They undergo various color changes: first pinkish and then powdery gray, maturing yellow-green, and attaining a reddish color in the autumn. The fruit is an acorn, which is relatively small, with a rounded tip, and greenish brown and held in a rough, woody cup.
Uses: Although acorns of the white oak are less bitter than those of other oak species, it is still recommended that they be treated before consumption to remove the tannins they contain. To do this, soak the nuts whole or crushed in boiling water with several rinsings and repeated boilings. Whole nuts can then be roasted to a delicious flavor, and the meal can be used in a variety of baked goods. Acorns are high in protein and fat and are an important source of food for wildlife as well.

Filaree, *Erodium cicutarium*
Dicots, family Geraniaceae
(geranium family)
Alternate name(s): Storksbill,
alfilaria
Size: To 12" tall
Range: Throughout the United States
Season: Flowers spring through summer
Habitat: Sunny, disturbed areas; roadsides
Description: Filaree is an introduced, small, herbaceous annual or
biennial related to the ornamental geranium plant. Its foliage is
concentrated about a basal rosette, with leaves that are soft, delicate, and pinnately divided, resembling the fronds of a fern. The
erect, often reddish, flowering stalks, with fine hairs, have few and
smaller leaves and terminate with a loose cluster of small, pink
to lavender, five-petaled flowers that begin blooming early in the
spring. The resulting fruit is a long, thin spike that resembles the
beak of a stork, hence the common name storksbill. When dry,
this fruit splits apart into five parts that curl up like a corkscrew,
helping the seed to penetrate into the soil.
Uses: The early, tender leaves are edible raw alone or in salads,
have a parsley-like flavor, and may also be cooked as a potherb
like spinach. The seeds are also edible, and the leaves have been
used medicinally as a tea.

Black Walnut, *Juglans nigra*
Dicots, family Juglandaceae
(walnut/hickory family)
Alternate name(s): American
black walnut
Size: To 90' tall
Range: Eastern United States
Season: Flowers in spring, nuts late summer and autumn
Habitat: Mixed deciduous woodlands, disturbed areas
Description: The black walnut is a native, deciduous, large, woody tree with a strong taproot and an open, rounded crown. The bark of mature trees is dark brown or grayish with deep furrows. Leaves are large, dark green, and pinnately compound with oval to lanceolate, prominently ribbed leaflets with serrate margins. Leaves may be up to 20" long and have over twenty leaflets, and they have a distinct, musty odor. Male flowers are in drooping catkins, whereas female flowers form clusters in the leaf axils and produce a spherical, green fruit. Walnut trees can propagate by their seeds or vegetatively from shoots (suckers) arising from the trunk.
Uses: Collect the fruits as they fall to the ground and remove the fleshy green coating and thick husk. The nuts therein are high in protein and oil and are edible raw or can be roasted or used in baking. Walnut is an important food source for wildlife, and the dark wood is prized for woodworking.

Wild Mint, *Mentha arvensis*
Dicots, family Lamiaceae/Labiatae
(mint family)
Alternate name(s): Field mint
Size: To 30" tall
Range: Most of the United States except for southeastern states
Season: Flowers summer through autumn
Habitat: Wet areas, meadows, stream sides
Description: The wild mint is a native to North America, among many introduced and naturalized varieties of mint. It is an herbaceous, erect annual with squared stems typical of the mint family, with opposite leaves that are ovate with pointed ends and toothed margins. The tiny, bell-shaped flowers are white, purple, or pink and occur in clusters at the leaf axils or terminally on the stem.
Uses: The fresh or dried leaves, seeped in hot water, make an aromatic tea that is soothing and can alleviate stomach upset. The leaves, rich in vitamins and minerals, also make a nice flavoring to salads, cooked dishes, and jellies.

Catnip, *Nepeta cataria*
Dicots, family Lamiaceae/Labitatae
(mint family)
Alternate name(s): Catmint
Size: To 30" tall
Range: Throughout the United States
Season: Flowers in summer
Habitat: Disturbed areas, fields, roadsides
Description: Catnip is an erect, perennial, bushy plant with many branches. The stem, like that of other members of the mint family, is four-sided and produces leaves opposite each other on the stem. The small, gray-green, cordate or arrow-shaped leaves have a toothed margin and are coated with fine, fuzzy hairs, making them silky soft. Small clusters of white to pale purple flowers appear on spikes at the stem's tip. All foliage has a musky, minty scent.
Uses: The fresh leaves can be steeped in hot water for a soothing tea to promote relaxation. Dried leaves can be stored for later use, and the tea they make will be slightly milder. Catnip is also a great treat for cats, of course! It contains chemicals, including nepetalactone, that are a strong attractant for cats.

Chia, *Salvia columbariae*
Dicots, family Lamiaceae/
Labiatae (mint family)
Alternate name(s): Chia sage
Size: To 18" tall
Range: Southwestern United States
Season: Flowers spring through summer
Habitat: Sunny, dry areas; chaparral, coastal scrub
Description: Chia is an herbaceous, erect, annual member of the mint family, native to Mexico and the southwestern United States. The foliage is soft and hairy. Leaves are mostly basal, forming a rosette of pinnately divided, lobed, crinkly leaflets. The stem is square in cross-section, rises above the rosette, and produces round clumps of tiny blue flowers at intervals that resemble small, blue pom-poms. The dried seeds can be knocked from the clusters fairly easily and collected in baskets.
Uses: Chia seeds have an ancient history of use since the times of the Aztecs. They can be mixed into a glass of water (add lemon and honey for flavor), where they will expand and make a delicious gelatinous drink known for its energy-giving qualities. The roasted seeds can be ground into flour, used whole for baked goods, or added to salads and shakes. Chia is now marketed commercially for its health benefits.

Mallow, *Malva neglecta*
Dicots, family Malvaceae
(mallow family)
Alternate name(s): Cheeseweed,
buttonweed
Size: To 3' tall
Range: Throughout the United States
Season: Flowers in spring and summer, fruit summer through autumn
Habitat: Disturbed areas, fields, gardens
Description: Mallow is an annual, bushy, or creeping herbaceous plant with a long, tenacious taproot. Its foliage is covered with small, stellate hairs, giving it a soft, fuzzy feel. The leaves are rounded with a wavy, crenate margin, palmate venation, and a petiole that joins near the center of the leaf. The flowers are small and white to light purple and have five petals. The common name of cheeseweed is derived from the fact that the little, pealike fruits look like tiny rounds of cheese.
Uses: The leaves of mallow can be eaten raw in salads, although their texture is a bit fuzzy and glutinous. Cooking them will give a more palatable texture and flavor. Leaves are also used as a thickener for soups or cooked dishes and were used to make the original marshmallow candy. Native Americans made a tea of the plant to soothe skin ailments.

American Lotus, *Nelumbo lutea*
Dicots, family Nelumbonaceae (lotus family)
Alternate name(s): Nelumbo
Size: To 8' tall, including underwater stems
Range: Eastern United States, California
Season: Flowers in summer
Habitat: Ponds, slow-moving streams, calm waters
Description: The American lotus is a large, perennial, aquatic plant native to the southeastern United States that bears a close resemblance to the water lily. It is quite large, with a spreading underground rhizome system up to 8' below the water's surface. The leaves unfurl to huge, circular disks, up to 2' across, that may float on the surface or rise into the air, assuming a bowl shape. The attachment of the petiole is in the middle of the leaf. Flowers are borne singly at the end of a long stalk that grows directly from the roots. They are among our largest flowers (about 10" wide), creamy white to yellow, with many petals and seeds that form in holes in a seedpod that looks like an inverted cone.
Uses: The young leaves of lotus make a good cooked green. The enlarged tubers along the rhizomes are edible, boiled or roasted like a potato, although they are difficult to procure in deep water. The immature and mature seeds are also edible roasted and make a tasty snack or can be ground into flour for baking.

Evening Primrose, *Denothera biennis*
Dicots, family Onagraceae
(evening primrose family)

Size: To 6' tall

Range: Primarily eastern United States

Season: Flowers summer through autumn

Habitat: Disturbed areas, roadsides, sunny meadows

Description: Evening primrose is a biennial, herbaceous plant that forms a basal rosette of ovate to lanceolate, dark green leaves with pale midribs during its first year. In the spring of the second year, an unbranched, erect stem grows with alternate, lanceolate leaves. The tip of the stem produces green flower buds and bright yellow, four-petaled flowers with drooping sepals. The flowers bloom a few at a time, opening in the evening and closing during the following morning. The seedpods are brownish, tubular structures that face upward and contain many small seeds.

Uses: The thick, long taproot is a delicious, somewhat spicy root vegetable, best when boiled to soften the taste and texture. Roots gathered during the spring of the first year are best. The basal leaves are tough and bitter, but leaves of the developing stalk are excellent as additions to salads or as a cooked green. The flower buds are tasty raw, and the flowers are flavorful and decorative added to dishes. The seeds are very nutritious, often marketed commercially, and can be eaten as a nutritional supplement.

Fireweed, *Epilbium angustifolium*
Dicots, family Onagraceae
(evening primrose family)
Alternate name(s): Willow herb
Size: To 6′ tall
Range: Throughout the United States
Season: Spring for shoots
Habitat: Disturbed areas, pastures, burned areas

Description: Fireweed is a perennial, erect, herbaceous plant native to North America that is a pioneer species that quickly colonizes recent burn areas and can reproduce by underground rhizomes. The stems are unbranched, smooth, and reddish. The leaves are alternate on the stem and lanceolate, with a smooth margin and curving venation. The small, four-petaled flowers appear in clusters terminally on the stem in a loose spike and are pink to fuchsia and based by a long, tubular pedicel. Upright, reddish seedpods contain many tiny seeds that can travel long distances through the air, held aloft by cottony hairs.

Uses: The young shoots and flowering stalks of fireweed can be cooked as a vegetable, and the young leaves can be used as a green in salads or cooked. Bitterness and toughness increase as the plant ages. The stems, peeled of the tough outer cuticle, are edible raw or cooked. The older leaves are often made into tea.

Wood Sorrel, *Oxalis stricta*
Dicots, family Oxalidaceae
(oxalis family)
Alternate name(s): Yellow sorrel,
shamrock
Size: To 12" tall
Range: Throughout the United
States
Season: Most seasons; may over-
winter in mild climates
Habitat: Woodlands, gardens

Description: Wood sorrel is a low-growing, delicate, herbaceous plant that superficially resembles a clover. It sprouts from seed or arises from an underground rhizome that buds at intervals and so often forms thick mats of plants. The leaves are alternate on the stem and consist of three heart-shaped leaflets that are green to reddish purple. Through each leaflet is a crease that allows the leaf to fold and bend. The flowers are bright yellow and occur in umbels. Seeds are formed in a long, thin, erect seedpod.

Uses: The leaves and upper stems of wood sorrel can be eaten raw, alone or in salads, and have a refreshing, tart taste. They can be cooked as well and turn a dark, dull green color. The flowers and seedpods are edible as well and can be prepared along with the leaves. An excellent tea, hot or chilled, can be made by steeping the dried or fresh leaves in hot water and adding a bit of honey. Although high in iron and vitamin C, wood sorrel should be used in moderation due to the presence of oxalates, which inhibit the availability of calcium in the body.

Common Plantain,
Plantago major
Dicots, family Plantagiaceae
(plantain family)
Alternate name(s): Goose
tongue, broadleaf plantain
Size: To 20" tall
Range: Throughout the
United States
Season: Flowers spring through autumn
Habitat: Disturbed areas, lawns, roadsides
Description: Common plantain is a widespread, introduced, herbaceous perennial plant. All leaves grow as dense basal rosettes of stalked, wide, oval leaves up to 8" long that have deep venation that tapers at both ends and smooth margins. The central, erect, leafless, flowering stalk emerges from this rosette and bears densely packed, tiny, pale greenish flowers along the upper part of its length. Looking closely, one can see that the stamens are purple. The similar and equally abundant *Plantago lanceolata* has narrow, pointed leaves.
Uses: The leaves of the common plantain are quite bitter but may be eaten raw if collected early in the season before the flowering stalk forms. Older leaves will be tough and stringy. Boiling or cooking into soups will make the leaves tender. The dried seeds have been a food since ancient times. Add them to salads or grind them into flour to use in baking. This plant has been dubbed white man's foot because it seems to have sprouted wherever early white settlers traveled.

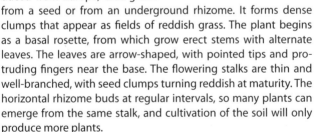

Sheep Sorrel, *Rumex acetosella*
Dicots, family Polygonaceae
(buckwheat family)
Alternate name(s): Field sorrel,
common sorrel, sour dock
Size: To 15" tall
Range: Throughout the United
States
Season: Flowers in summer
Habitat: Disturbed areas, gardens,
fields; prefers moist soil
Description: Sheep sorrel is a thin,
erect, herbaceous plant, introduced from Europe, that grows
from a seed or from an underground rhizome. It forms dense
clumps that appear as fields of reddish grass. The plant begins
as a basal rosette, from which grow erect stems with alternate
leaves. The leaves are arrow-shaped, with pointed tips and pro-
truding fingers near the base. The flowering stalks are thin and
well-branched, with seed clumps turning reddish at maturity. The
horizontal rhizome buds at regular intervals, so many plants can
emerge from the same stalk, and cultivation of the soil will only
produce more plants.
Uses: The young leaves from the basal rosette are best and have a
tart or sour flavor. They, along with the tender, early upper stalks,
can be eaten raw or boiled. The dried leaves and stems can be
steeped in hot water to make tea. Sheep sorrel should be con-
sumed in moderation due to the presence of oxalates, which
inhibit the absorption of some nutrients.

Curly Dock, *Rumex crispus*
Dicots, family Polygonaceae (buckwheat family)
Alternate name(s): Narrowleaf dock,
yellow dock
Size: To 4' tall
Range: Throughout the United States
Season: Flowers spring through autumn,
depending on region
Habitat: Disturbed areas, gardens,
roadsides
Description: Curly dock was introduced
from Europe but is now prevalent in
North America. It is an annual whose
roots overwinter and produce new
growth each spring. The plant starts as a basal rosette of dark
green, long-petioled, spoon-shaped leaves, from which emerge
one or more erect stems that support long and narrow, alternate
leaves with a wavy and curled margin. Where leaves attach to the
stem at nodes, there is a thin, papery sheath, characteristic of
members of the *Rumex* genus. Clusters of small buds form on the
flower stalks, and the whole plant begins turning brown in late
summer. The seeds are three-sided, shiny, and brown.
Uses: The young leaves of the basal rosette, before the erect stems
merge, are edible. Their flavor is mildly tart or bitter but good raw
mixed with other greens or boiled like spinach. The top of stems,
when buds are just forming, can be eaten raw or cooked. Curly
dock is high in nutrients but also contains some oxalates (which
inhibit the absorption of some minerals) and thus is best con-
sumed in moderation.

Pickerelweed, *Pontederia cordata*
Dicots, family Pontederiaceae
(water hyacinth family)
Size: To 36" tall
Range: Eastern United States
Season: Flowers through summer
Habitat: Ponds, slow-moving streams, freshwater marshes
Description: Pickerelweed is a native, perennial, herbaceous, aquatic plant that is fast-growing and can cover large areas. The plant is usually at least partially submerged, with leaves arising basally from the root. Leaves are quite large, to 10" long, with parallel venation, usually lanceolate, with a heart-shaped base, making them look like long arrowheads. The single flowering stalk is thick and terminates in a spike of small, sky-blue flowers that bloom successively up to the tip.
Uses: The young, tender leaves and leaf stalks of pickerelweed can be cooked as vegetables or eaten raw, chopped, in salads. The seeds are also edible raw or roasted.

Spring Beauty, *Claytonia virginica*
Dicots, family Portulaceae (purslane family)
Size: To 12" tall
Range: Eastern United States
Season: Flowers in spring only
Habitat: Mixed hardwood wood-
lands with rich, moist soils

Description: A perennial, delicate, herbaceous plant, spring beauty is one of a few similar native plants called spring beauty and found growing across North America. It appears only for a couple of months during the spring and may form extensive carpets across the forest floor. Several thin stems arise from an enlarged, rounded root called a corm. Each stem has two opposite, narrowly elliptical leaves with smooth margins and ends in a loose cluster of several beautiful, white or pinkish, five-petaled flowers that have thin, darker veins. Each year the corm grows a bit larger and will support more stems the following spring.

Uses: Spring beauty is best known for the enlarged roots, called fairy spuds, which grow several inches deep in the soil. They are best harvested before or after foliage growth but may be difficult to find. They can be used somewhat like a small potato: boiled, roasted, mashed, or even eaten raw. They have a delicious, delicate, sweet chestnut flavor. The greens are also edible raw in salads or cooked as a potherb.

Miner's Lettuce, *Montia perfoliata*
or *Claytonia perfoliata*
Dicots, family Portulaceae (purslane family)
Alternate name(s): Winter purlane
Size: To 12" tall, usually smaller
Range: Western United States
Season: Flowers early spring through summer
Habitat: Cool, moist areas in foothills or low mountainous areas
Description: Miner's lettuce is a fleshy, delicate, herbaceous annual with single, long stems that emerge from a basal rosette. The basal leaves and early leaves on the stems are oval or lanceolate in shape, whereas mature leaves rise on tall petioles and are quite round. Above these leaves rise several tiny, five-petaled, white or pale pink flowers. The resulting small, black seeds are an important food source for birds and small mammals.
Uses: Native Americans and early settlers (including miners, of course) ate the fleshy, tender leaves as a salad, and the plant gave them an important supply of vitamin C. The leaves are also good lightly cooked. They have a subtle taste with a pleasant texture, making them a good base for mixing with bitter greens, onions, and herbs. They are best harvested when young because the older, reddish leaves can be quite dry.

Purslane, *Portulaca oleraceae*
Dicots, family Portulaceae
(purslane family)
Alternate name(s): Verdolaga,
pusley
Size: Sprawling to 2′ wide
Range: Throughout the United States
Season: Summer for leaves, late autumn for seeds
Habitat: Disturbed areas, gardens
Description: Purslane is a fleshy, small, heat-loving, annual, herbaceous plant that is widely distributed and occurs in most yards
as a weed. It branches close to the ground and creeps outward
on tubular, smooth, pinkish stems. The leaves are small, succulent, spatula-shaped with broad, rounded tips, and are arranged
opposite or in rosettes. The flower is small, yellow-green, and
short-lived. If fertilized, the flower will mature into a little cup with
tiny black seeds. Bits of the stems, if chopped up into the soil, will
resprout to form new plants.
Uses: The leaves of purslane are delicious raw eaten in salads,
cooked as spinach, or added to baked dishes. The stems can be
eaten as the leaves or pickled with vinegar and sugar. The seeds
can be threshed from the husks when dry and ground into a nutritious flour for baking. Purslane is very nutritious and contains vitamin E, iron, and antioxidants.

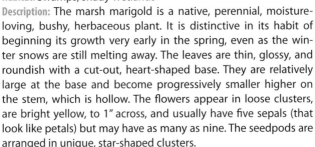

Marsh Marigold, *Caltha palustris*
Dicots, family Ranunculaceae
(buttercup family)
Alternate name(s): Cowslip, kingcup
Size: To 28" tall
Range: Midwestern and northeastern
United States
Season: Flowers in spring
Habitat: Swamps, shady wetlands

Description: The marsh marigold is a native, perennial, moisture-loving, bushy, herbaceous plant. It is distinctive in its habit of beginning its growth very early in the spring, even as the winter snows are still melting away. The leaves are thin, glossy, and roundish with a cut-out, heart-shaped base. They are relatively large at the base and become progressively smaller higher on the stem, which is hollow. The flowers appear in loose clusters, are bright yellow, to 1" across, and usually have five sepals (that look like petals) but may have as many as nine. The seedpods are arranged in unique, star-shaped clusters.

Uses: The young basal leaves and flower buds of the marsh marigold can be boiled and eaten as a potherb or vegetable. They should never be eaten raw because all parts of this plant contain a somewhat toxic chemical that can cause skin irritation and illness. Boiling them in water neutralizes this toxin and renders the foliage perfectly edible. The rather bland flavor is enhanced by adding butter and salt. Native cultures also used the root for medicinal purposes.

Western Serviceberry,

Amelanchier pallida
Dicots, family Rosaceae (rose family)
Size: To 20' tall
Range: Western United States
Season: Flowers in spring, berries in summer
Habitat: Arid foothills, higher elevations, disturbed areas

Description: The western serviceberry is one of many members of this often-overlooked group of plants. It is a perennial, woody shrub or small tree with a fruit that ripens relatively early in the season. The bark is smooth and pale gray. The leaves are alternate on branches, oval with pointed tips and finely serrate margins. Flowers are up to 1" wide, bloom early, have five thin, white petals, and are borne loosely on spikes. Berries are round, beginning greenish, then red, and eventually becoming a deep, dark purple.

Uses: Berries can be harvested throughout the summer, eaten as is or dried for a tasty food later in the year. Natives often mixed the dried fruit with meat for a kind of pemmican. Berries are also good in baked dishes, especially pies, and are used in jams and jellies. Serviceberries are an important food for wildlife and a favorite of bears.

Wood Strawberry,

Fragaria vesca
Dicots, family Rosaceae (rose family)

Size: To 6" tall

Range: Throughout the United States except the far Southeast

Season: Flowers in spring, fruit in summer

Habitat: Moist, shaded woodlands

Description: The wood strawberry is a small, low-growing, herbaceous, perennial plant that looks similar to the cultivated strawberry. All leaves arise from hairy, basal stalks that emerge from a root crown, and the plant propagates from nodes along underground runners. The leaves are divided into three oval leaflets with serrate margins. The flower stalk often grows higher than the leaves and bears a small cluster of white, five-petaled flowers. The fruit is a small, compact, red berry, with seeds adhering to the outside surface.

Uses: Delicious and similar in appearance to commercial strawberries but smaller, the berries are edible right off the plant or may be dried for later consumption. They also have many uses in cooked and baked goods, pies, and jams. A tea, high in nutrients and vitamin C, can be made with the dried or fresh leaves.

Chokecherry, *Prunus virginiana*
Dicots, family Rosaceae (rose family)
Size: To 15' tall
Range: Northern United States
Season: Flowers spring through summer, fruit in autumn
Habitat: Fields, stream sides, disturbed areas
Description: The chokecherry is a widespread, native, large shrub or treelike perennial with thornless foliage. The leaves are arranged alternately on the stems, have a thin petiole, are ovate with a pointed tip, and have finely serrate margins. The bark is gray and mostly smooth except for small, raised, lens-shaped bumps. The flowers are white and five-petaled and appear in tight clusters. The small, roundish berries are first red, then mature to a deep blackish purple, and occur in clumps as the flowers.
Uses: The fresh berries are very astringent if underripe, so they should be collected after they turn dark purple, even after the first frost of autumn. The longer they stay on the plant, the sweeter they will become. Jams and jellies can be make by cooking the fresh berries and straining out the juice. The berries are also very good dried and eaten as is or mixed with cereal.

Common Wild Rose,

Rosa virginiana
Dicots, family Rosaceae (rose family)
Alternate name(s): Virginia rose
Size: To 5' tall
Range: Eastern United States
Season: Flowers in summer, fruit in autumn
Habitat: Quite variable; dry fields, creek sides, disturbed areas
Description: This is one of many species of wild roses, all of which share similar characteristics. The common wild rose is a perennial, prickly shrub with woody stems that have hooked spines and produce leaves in an alternate arrangement. The leaves are divided pinnately into seven or nine ovate leaflets with serrate margins. The flowers are five-petaled, about 2" wide, and colored pale to rich pink. The fruit is called a hip—a shiny, smooth, red globe that persists on the plant through the winter. Leaves become brown to reddish in the autumn.
Uses: The leaves are edible, have a mild flavor, and can be eaten alone or as a nice addition to salads. A syrup or jelly can be made by boiling the hips in water, straining the juice, and adding sugar and lemon. The flowers are edible as well and can be a decorative part of salads. A flavorful tea can be made by steeping the leaves, petals, or hips in water. The hips are very high in vitamin C.

Thimbleberry, *Rubus parviflorus*
Dicots, family Rosaceae (rose family)
Size: To 8' tall
Range: Western and northern
United States
Season: Flowers in summer, fruit
summer through early autumn
Habitat: Foothills, higher-elevation open woodlands, stream sides, disturbed areas
Description: The thimbleberry is a sprawling, well-branched, peren-nial shrub that sometimes forms dense stands by propagating by means of underground rhizomes. The bark of older stems is gray or reddish and peeling, and the stems are thornless, unlike most members of the rose family. The leaves are soft and hairy, light green, large, palmate with lobes, have a serrate margin, and resemble those of a maple tree. Large flowers grow scattered on the branches, are five-petaled, and are white or pale pink with a yellow interior. The "berry," actually a cluster of small fruits, becomes rosy red when ripe. When it is picked, there is a hollow center, similar in shape to a thimble or our common raspberry.
Uses: The ripe berries are wonderful eaten right off the bush, although they can be quite tart. The berries also make an excellent jam. The young shoots can be eaten raw or cooked as a vegetable.

Pacific Blackberry,

Rubus ursinus
Dicots, family Rosaceae
(rose family)
Alternate name(s): California blackberry, bramble, dewberry
Size: Stems to 8' long
Range: Western United States
Season: Flowers and fruit in summer
Habitat: Sunny areas, disturbed areas, creek sides
Description: The Pacific blackberry is one of many species of blackberry that are subtly different from one another. It is a perennial, bushy, prickly, trailing bramble that forms dense thickets of foliage and arching stems. Its unruly growth and fierce spines are in contrast to the sweet, juicy fruits. Stems are tough and lined with sharp spines. The trifoliate leaves are arranged alternately and have leaflets that are prickly with serrate margins. The flowers are white with five thin petals and appear in clusters. The fruit begins red but soon turns a deep, blackish purple and consists of a compact group of drupes (so it is not technically considered a berry).
Uses: The fruits, right off the bush when dark and ripe, are sweet, juicy, and flavorful. They can also be dried and later reconstituted with water. The young shoots can be cooked and eaten as a vegetable, and the leaves and roots can be made into a tea. Blackberries are an important food source for animals, and the thickets make excellent cover.

Goosegrass, *Galium aparine*
Dicots, family Rubiaceae (madder family)
Alternate name(s): Cleavers, stickywilly,
common bedstraw
Size: Stems sprawl to 5' long
Range: Throughout United States
Season: Flowers spring through
summer
Habitat: Disturbed areas, gardens,
woodlands

Description: Goosegrass is an herbaceous, annual, sprawling plant native to North America with sticky, Velcro-like foliage. The stems are very long, thin, four-sided, and lined with downcurved, hooked prickles. They are fairly weak and rely on support from other plants or fences. The leaves are small, lanceolate, prickled, grow at nodes in the stem, and are arranged in whorls of six to eight. Tiny white or greenish, four-petaled flowers grow in loose clusters from a pedicel coming out to the leaf axils and mature into round, bristly fruits.

Uses: Considered a noxious weed by most gardeners because of its tendency to overtake other plants, goosegrass is also a fine edible plant. The young stems and leaves can be eaten if boiled first to lessen the prickly texture of the flesh. Also, the mature fruits, roasted, can be brewed as a coffee-type beverage.

Pasture Gooseberry, *Ribes cynosbati*
Dicots, family Saxifagaceae (saxifrage family)
Alternate name(s): Prickly gooseberry, dogberry
Size: To 4' tall
Range: Midwestern and eastern United States
Season: Flowers late spring, fruit summer through autumn
Habitat: Dry soils in open woodlands
Description: The pasture gooseberry is a perennial, moderately branching, deciduous shrub, closely related to the currant plant. The older stems are grayish and woody, whereas younger stems and branches are green and covered with short, thin thorns that are less abundant on very thin stems. At the branch nodes are one or more much longer thorns. The leaves are alternate on the stem, palmately divided into three or five cordate lobes that have a crenated or round-toothed margin. The flowers are small, drooping, yellowish green, and occur in small clusters. The fruit is a globe-shaped berry with fleshy spines, beginning green and ripening to reddish purple.
Uses: Gooseberries are high in vitamin C, can be eaten as is or cooked to be made into pies, jams, or fruit leather. They are also a nice flavoring to juices and teas.

Mullein, *Verbascum thapsus*
Dicots, family Scrophulariaceace
(figwort family)
Size: To 6' tall
Range: Throughout the United
States
Season: Flowers spring through
autumn
Habitat: Disturbed areas, dry fields
Description: Mullein is a native, herbaceous biennial that forms a basal rosette of leaves during its first year and an erect stem during its second year. The basal leaves are quite large, elliptical to spoon-shaped, light green, and covered with fine hairs, making the leaves very soft to the touch. Toward the apex of the stalk, leaves become smaller and grow upright against the stem, eventually merging with a stout, cylindrical flower cluster. A few at a time, bright yellow, five-petaled flowers appear on the spike, maturing into small, brownish seeds.
Uses: The primary use of mullein has been a tea made out of fresh or dried leaves to relieve congestion of the lungs. Native Americans smoked the dried leaves for the same benefit. It is sometimes called, quite irreverently, cowboy's toilet paper because of the soft, papery nature of the leaves.

Carrion-Flower, *Symphytum officinale*
Dicots, family Smilacaceae (catbrier family)
Alternate name(s): Smilax, Jacob's ladder
Size: Vines to 8′ long
Range: Central and eastern United States
Season: Flowers in spring, fruit in autumn
Habitat: Moist woodlands, thickets, meadows
Description: Carrion-flower is an herbaceous, perennial, fast-growing, climbing vine that has separate male and female plants. The stems are smooth, without thorns, and have long, curling tendrils that cling to trunks or fences for support. The leaves arise alternately on long petioles and are ovate to somewhat cordate, with parallel venation and smooth margins. Small, greenish flowers, scented like carrion, form in umbels from the leaf axils in both male and female plants. The staminate (female) flowers produce clusters of juicy, round, dark blue berries with a pale, powdery coating.
Uses: Despite its off-putting common name, carrion-flower is a pleasant, edible plant. The tips of young shoots, while still tender, make a good cooked vegetable that is very similar in form and taste to asparagus. The leaves are also edible, cooked as greens. The roots are useful as a thickening agent in cooked dishes and soups.

Nasturtium, *Tropaeolum majus*
Dicots, family Tropaleoaceae
(nasturtium family)
Size: Climbs to 6' tall
Range: Throughout the United
States
Season: Flowers in spring
through autumn or in winter in
mild climates
Habitat: Disturbed areas, sunny
fields

Description: The nasturtium is a perennial or annual, hardy, fast-growing plant introduced from South America, grown as an ornamental for its showy flowers but often found growing in the wild. It has a creeping or climbing, vinelike nature on stems that can twist up fences or trellises. The leaves are large, bright green and round or shield-shaped, and arise from a long petiole that attaches at a leaf's center. The flowers are brightly colored shades of orange or yellow (sometimes red), usually with five petals, and have a long, nectar-containing spur on the underside. The seeds, left to dry and fall away, will easily produce more plants the following season.

Uses: Both flowers and leaves of the nasturtium are edible as greens, usually mixed into a salad. The flowers are a nice decorative edible and can also be stuffed for an appetizer. The green seedpods are edible as is or pickled like capers. Although it is not related to the watercress, *Nasturtium officinale,* the two plants do have a similar peppery flavor.

Siberian Elm, *Ulmus pumila*
Dicots, family Ulmacae
(elm family)
Alternate name(s): Dwarf elm
Size: To 65' tall
Range: Midwestern United States
Season: Flowers in early spring
Habitat: Disturbed areas, fields, vacant urban lots
Description: The Siberian elm is an introduced tree from Asia. It is a medium-size, hardy, deciduous tree with an open crown and light gray-brown, coarsely furrowed bark. Leaves are alternate on the branches, dark green, and elliptical, with pointed tips and serrate margins. The flowers are greenish, in small clusters, and produce thin, disklike, one-seeded pods called samaras. These fruits dry and fall to the ground or are carried some distance by the wind. This elm was initially cultivated as a fast-growing windbreak or shade tree and is considered by some to be undesirable because of its invasive nature and likelihood to become diseased.
Uses: The young samara, before it is dry and brittle, is a tasty, nut-like food that can be eaten raw. Dried samaras can be winnowed, leaving just the seeds, which can be eaten raw or used in cooked dishes, somewhat like a small, flat bean.

Nettle, *Urtica dioica*
Dicots, family Urticaceae
(nettle family)
Alternate name(s): Stinging nettle
Size: To 4' tall
Range: Throughout the United States
Season: Flowers in summer
Habitat: Disturbed areas, roadsides, moist areas
Description: Nettle is a perennial, herbaceous, erect plant with mostly unbranched, four-sided stems. The leaves are opposite on the stem, stalked, lanceolate to ovate, with serrate margins. The stem and leaves are covered with short, stinging hairs containing histamine and formic acid, which causes a mild to severe burning sensation and rash on the skin. Thin, greenish flower clusters grow from the axils of the upper leaves. Nettle may form dense groups of plants by means of creeping, underground rhizomes.
Uses: The leaves of nettle, high in vitamins C and A, can be eaten by boiling or drying them first—either method will render the stinging action inert. The tender, growing top of the shoots is also edible, cooked like asparagus. The fibrous stems have been used by Native Americans to make twine or fishing nets.

Bird's Foot Violet, *Viola pedata*

Dicots, family Violaceae (violet family)

Size: To 8" tall

Range: Midwestern and eastern United States

Season: Flowers spring through early summer

Habitat: Dry woodlands, roadsides, fields, sunny areas

Description: Bird's foot violet is a native, annual, herbaceous plant. The delicate leaves are basal, arising on short to long petioles, palmately divided into long, thin, oblong lobes that are reminiscent of a bird's foot (hence the common name). The comparatively large, to 1½" wide, flowers have fine, violet-blue petals that become paler near the base, with the lowermost petal having a spur emerging from the back. The central stamens are orange, and lateral petals do not have bearding, as do those of other violet species.

Uses: The young leaves of bird's foot violet are edible mixed with salad greens or cooked as spinach. They can also be added to other cooked dishes as a thickening agent (bird's foot violet is sometimes referred to as wild okra). The leaves can be made into tea, and the flowers are decorative additions to food or used to make a fragrant candy. Some violets are rare or endangered, so it is best to harvest them in moderation.

Index

About the Author/Illustrator

Todd Telander is a naturalist, illustrator, and artist living in Walla Walla, Washington. He has studied and illustrated wildlife since 1989, while living in California, Colorado, New Mexico, and Washington. He graduated from the University of California at Santa Cruz with degrees in biology, environmental studies, and scientific illustration and has since illustrated numerous books and other publications, including FalconGuides' Scats and Tracks series. His wife, Kirsten Telander, is a writer, and he has two sons, Miles and Oliver. His work can be viewed online at www.toddtelander.com.